EXPLORING
BUSINESS
AND
ECONOMICS

The Stock Market

Fred Barbash

Chelsea House Publishers
Philadelphia

Frontis: The New York Stock Exchange stands on Wall Street in lower Manhattan.

CHELSEA HOUSE PUBLISHERS

EDITOR IN CHIEF Sally Cheney
DIRECTOR OF PRODUCTION Kim Shinners
PRODUCTION MANAGER Pamela Loos
ART DIRECTOR Sara Davis

Choptank Syndicate/Chestnut Productions

EDITORIAL Norman Macht and Mary Hull
PRODUCTION Lisa Hochstein
PICTURE RESEARCH Norman Macht

http://www.chelseahouse.com

First Printing

1 3 5 7 9 8 6 4 2

Library of Congress Cataloging-in-Publication Data

Barbash, Fred.
    The stock market / Fred Barbash
    p. cm. – (Exploring business and economics)
    ISBN 0-7910-6639-8 (alk. paper)
1. Stock exchanges. I. Title. II. Series.
HG4551.B37 2001
332.64'2—dc21   2001042514

Table of Contents

1 The Markets   7

2 Going Public   15

3 Stocks in the Investing Universe   25

4 How Investors Buy and Sell Stocks   33

5 Looking for Growth   41

6 Navigating the Stock Market   49

   Glossary   60

   Further Reading   62

   Index   63

It is a Wall Street tradition for businessmen and women to touch the bronze bull that stands in the financial district of New York. The bull symbolizes a bull market, in which stock prices go up.

The Markets

As the 21st century began, half the households in the United States had an immediate stake in the nation's **stock markets.** They owned **stocks** directly or through **mutual funds.** Many millions more depended on the markets for their retirement through employer-sponsored pension plans heavily invested in stocks.

This represented a big change in people's lives. Not very long ago, almost everyone who retired depended on a pension (money paid to them each month after their working days were over) from their former employer, a union, or the government. Few people could afford to live as well as they had when they were working and had a steady income. But a booming stock market, especially in the last 10 years of the 20th century, changed all that. For the first time, people's investments in the stock market were worth more than the value of their homes. Thus the stock market took on increasing meaning in their lives. Today, millions of people who are retiring from their jobs have more money to spend than their parents or grandparents ever dreamed of.

So vast have these holdings become, when the market's doing well, people feel more prosperous, whether or not they really are. When people feel prosperous, they spend more freely on homes, cars, vacations, and consumer goods. This "wealth effect" pumps up the economy.

The **Internet** and online trading also opened up access to individual stocks to millions of investors who previously had invested only in mutual funds. As recently as the 1980s, investors could not buy individual stocks without paying commissions of $200 or more. This was too expensive for people of ordinary means. It was also a struggle to find a broker who would deal in small lots of shares—25 or 50 or even 100 shares. By 1999 investors could trade up to 1,000 shares of a stock for as little as $7.

Bull, Bear, or Crash?

Bull markets, bear markets, and **crashes** are good news, bad news, and terrible news. In a bull market, most stock prices are going up. In a bear market, they are going down. In a crash, they go down in a hurry. The two largest crashes occurred in 1929 and 1987. The first led to the **Great Depression.** The second preceded the greatest period of economic growth in American history.

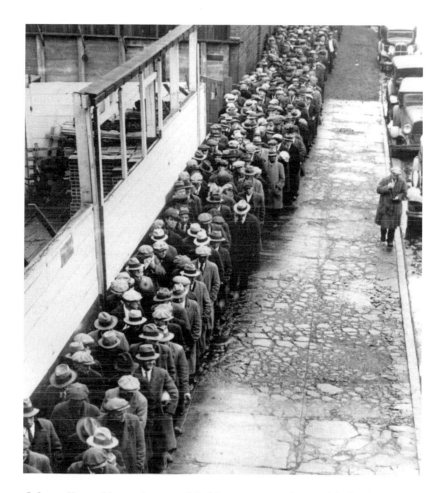

A long line of homeless and jobless men wait outside in the cold for a free meal at New York's municipal lodging house in the winter of 1932–33. In the years following the stock market crash of 1929, bank failures wiped out the savings of millions of Americans, and businesses closed, putting people out of work.

Online trading is simple to do. An investor opens an account by sending in a certain amount of money, often about $2,000. He gets an account number and a password to log in. Without further ado, he can begin buying stocks. It seems speedy. Click the mouse. Buy a stock. Click again. Sell a stock. But trade execution (completion) is no faster

Online Trading Academy.Com employees demonstrate online trading during the second annual International Online Trading Expo in Ontario, California, in 2000. As many as 99,000 shares were traded in 15 minutes, yielding a profit of $6,300.

than the system's capacity to process orders. Orders to buy and sell wait in line for anywhere from 30 seconds to 30 minutes or longer, depending on how active the market is. A price may change during this time lag so that the price on the computer screen when placing the order may not be the price at which it is filled.

Until the mid 1970s, the only way to purchase stocks was through so-called full service brokers who offered investing advice and sometimes tried to sell the investment products sponsored by their companies. Starting in 1975, the Charles Schwab Company broke the domination of the full service brokers, by opening a discount **brokerage.** By offering less advice or research, Schwab was able to lower the fees they charged their customers.

In the mid-1990s, online interactive communications hit the scene. Among the first commercial uses of the Internet was stock trading at a deep discount level. New companies were able to cut commissions even further than Schwab by offering only trading, no advice, and no human contact. Computers could do everything.

Online trading took the country by storm in part because of the low cost and in part because it coincided with the bull market in technology. By 2000, some 10 million people had Internet-based brokerage accounts with one of about 100 companies in the field. Individual investors became a powerful force in the market. A few went to the extreme of quitting jobs and becoming **day traders,** buying and selling numerous stocks in a single day.

The subject of online trading is controversial. Some professionals believe it's similar to turning a small child loose in a candy store. It makes trading too easy, they say, encouraging too much trading and impulsive decisions. Eventually, many of the large brokerage houses that had criticized online trading offered it to customers in order to remain competitive.

Keeping Up With The Financial News

The world's leading financial newspapers are *The Wall Street Journal* and *The Financial Times. Investors Business Daily* focuses heavily on the stock market. Useful magazines for investors include *Fortune, Barron's, Business Week,* and *SmartMoney. Money* magazine specializes in reporting about mutual funds.

Thomas Edison invented the ticker tape machine, which transmitted stock prices and printed them out on thin pieces of paper. Today stock prices are transmitted electronically onto computer screens.

But that's not the whole story. Thousands of publicly traded corporations, representing trillions of dollars of the country's output, also have an interest in the stock market. Their ability to grow and prosper depends in whole or in part on their ability to raise money through the markets. They use stock as if it were cash, paying their employees with it, and using it to acquire other companies.

State and federal governments also watch the markets. The more profits people make, the more taxes the government will collect. This is because investors pay taxes on **dividends** and profits from the sale of stocks. When the market goes down and people are not making money, the government is poorer.

For better or for worse, market indicators such as the **Dow Jones Industrial Average (the Dow),** the **North American Securities Dealers Automated Quotation System (NASDAQ),** and the **Standard and Poor 500 (S&P 500)** have become the symbol of the wealth of the nation. It's as if some great wealthometer is taking a reading every second of every day the stock market is open.

The accuracy of the reading is questionable. The behavior of investors is often emotional rather than rational. They buy and sell based on what they think might happen, with no way of knowing what will happen. The only sure thing is that surprises will occur. The stock market rolls up and down like a roller coaster, and nobody knows when it will reach the top or the bottom each time it changes direction. Like the rides at an amusement park, it can frighten investors when it's racing downhill, and excite them when it's climbing.

New companies go public all the time. Stock in Krispy Kreme Doughnuts, Inc., was traded on the floor of the New York Stock Exchange for the first time on May 17, 2001. Krispy Kreme Doughnuts opened its first day of trading on a sweet note, with its stock gaining more than 5 percent.

Going Public

American folklore is filled with stories of businesses born in garages that went on to become giants of industry. Some of these stories are at least close to the truth. Henry Ford really did start his car business by tinkering with farm machinery in a barn. Hewlett Packard and Apple, leaders of new computer technology, were begun in garages by entrepreneurs with very low budgets. The spark of creativity may be ignited anywhere and anytime.

Yet, without enough money to develop it, an idea may remain only an idea. We can build better mousetraps, write better software, design better cars, and dream the impossible dream. But for new companies and old companies, it always takes money to make possible the impossible.

The world's **capital** (another word for money) markets are the great matchmakers in this story. They bring together those in need of money with people who have money to invest.

Without a ready source of capital, an otherwise great business can wither. The stock market is part of a vast system that allocates capital globally. Companies may borrow money from banks or from investors by selling **bonds.** They may obtain money from a group of people who are willing to finance a new venture in exchange for ownership of a piece of the business. The risks can also be large in a new company, but the rewards if the company succeeds are always greater.

Another way to raise money is by selling shares of **common stock** to the public. Each share of stock represents ownership of a portion of the company. Issuing stock begins with an **initial public offering (IPO).** This is also known as a company "going public." This means exactly what it suggests. Taking a company public involves offering shares of the company to people on the outside, anyone able and willing to buy them for the first time.

Before going public, a company must file a report called a **prospectus,** along with many other papers, with the **Securities and Exchange Commission (SEC).** The SEC is the United States government regulatory agency responsible for overseeing the investment industry. The prospectus describes the work of the company and the risks of buying its stocks. Typically, the prospectus sounds horrible. It must state the worst that can happen to a company: it might not make much money; it might be uncompetitive; it might collapse in a heap. On the one hand these warnings are

Dow Jones Industrial Average
Monthly Data (1896–2001)

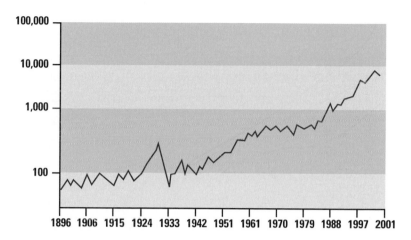

This shows the growth of the value of stocks as represented by the Dow Jones Industrial Average, commonly called the Dow. The Dow represents a basket of 30 of the leading corporations. Its components have changed over the years, reflecting changes in industry and the economy.

slightly unreal for many solid companies going public; on the other hand, they are all possibilities and should be taken seriously. Publicly traded companies can and do go out of business, leaving a stockholder with a worthless investment.

People who agree to put their money into a new business expect to see profitable results. Sometimes that takes time and patience. When Henry Ford began making automobiles 100 years ago, he built fine racing cars to test his engines. They won races. That attracted investors. Henry Ford spent the money improving his cars, but he didn't sell any. He said they weren't good enough yet. When he needed more money, he had a hard time finding new backers. The word had gotten around that Henry Ford spent too much time and money perfecting his cars and not enough trying to sell them. It took a few years before he was ready to make cars to sell. Then his cars became the biggest sellers for many years.

The Ford Motor Company remained a private, family-owned business until 1956, when it sold stock to the public for the first time. It was a huge, successful company when the Ford Foundation sold 10 million shares. Ford is one of the few examples of a company going public in order to diversify its investments. Unlike Ford, most companies go public because they need to raise more capital in order to expand.

Prior to the IPO, company executives travel around describing their company to professional investment managers. This helps them see how much interest there is among investors. The greater the interest, the higher the company can price the shares.

The price of those first shares sold in the IPO is a critical moment in a company's fortunes. Many people don't realize it, but the only money a company obtains from the sale of stock comes from the first sale—through the IPO. If it sells 10 million shares for $10 each, the company gets $100 million, minus the fees paid to investment bankers.

Initial Public Offerings

Initial Public Offerings—IPOs—created great excitement in the late 1990s as one after another new technology companies went public and then watched their stock value double or triple. Some called it IPO fever. It cooled off by 2001 when almost all of these companies experienced financial trouble, some of them going out of business for good.

Wall Street in lower New York City has been the financial center of the world for more than 100 years. This is how it looked on a quiet day when horse-drawn wagons were still sharing the streets with automobiles, and everybody wore a hat in the winter time.

Once the stock is sold, it gets a ticker symbol—initials meant to stand for the company—and becomes available for purchase by the general public. The buying and selling of shares after the IPO takes place is between buyers and sellers in an **aftermarket** or secondary market. The company gets nothing directly from aftermarket trading. It's as if you sell a car to someone who then sells it to someone

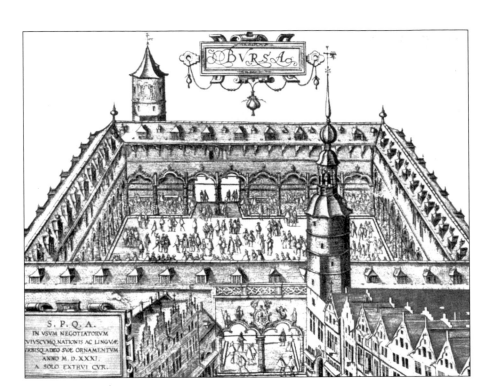

The stock market is not an American invention. This marketplace, called the Bourse, in Antwerp, Belgium, was built in the 15th century.

else. You get the money from the first sale, but nothing from the second. The stock market that everyone watches is a secondary market. This market is not a place but an activity, the trading of shares among investors. Shares of most large companies in the United States are listed on one of three stock exchanges: the **New York Stock Exchange (NYSE),** the North American Securities Dealers Automated Quotation system (NASDAQ), and the American Stock Exchange (ASE). Other companies trade in a smaller "over the counter bulletin board" market.

Stock exchanges are centralized systems through which potential buyers and sellers of shares participate in a giant auction. Through an exchange, buyers declare what they're willing to pay to acquire a share while the sellers state the price they will accept to part with it. When they get close, a market price is reached at which the stock may change hands. An investor willing to buy or sell at the market price can almost always do so in this marketplace. This is important. If people thought they might never be able to sell their stocks, few would ever buy them.

Brokers who act as agents for the public keep the whole system running. The stock market is not the sort of market anyone can just walk into and pick goods off the shelf. The investor must go through a broker—a company licensed to handle trades and keep investor accounts. The brokerage company itself may send the order through yet another company that processes trades. Many millions of investors own stock indirectly by buying shares of mutual funds. Mutual funds pool the money of large numbers of people and buy stocks on their behalf for a fee. These companies are only a part of the vast business called the financial services industry.

For most of the history of the stock markets in America, shares have been priced in fractions—$10\frac{1}{8}$, $10\frac{3}{8}$ and so forth. This tradition came from old metal coins that could be divided into eight pieces. The markets began gradually converting to decimals in 2000 so that $10\frac{1}{8}$ would be

Buying Shares in a Business

If you own even one share of a company like Wal-Mart, Kellogg, or Coca-Cola, or any other large business, you really are a part-owner of the entire business. Someone who owns one million shares of a company that has 10 million shares outstanding owns 10 percent of the business. It doesn't matter if you own only one share, you are still a part-owner of the entire company.

stated as $10.13. Today all shares are priced in dollars and cents.

The prices of individual stocks move up and down according to what investors think about the companies' future prospects. When a lot of people want to buy a stock, investors already holding it demand a higher price and the price goes up. When people are more inclined to sell a stock they own, buyers will seek lower prices, driving the price down.

Usually, but not always, interest in a company rises and falls as people try to guess its future growth. But common sense and accurate predictions of the future do not rule the market. Emotions have a lot to do with the decisions people make.

Manias such as the interest in Internet companies during the late 1990s come and go. Panic selling, driven by fear, occurs from time to time, sometimes scaring people away from stocks for years. After the stock market crash of 1929, millions of Americans wouldn't go near the markets for decades. Events having no obvious relation to the stock market, such as fears of military conflicts, or the president becoming ill, may cause heavy buying and selling.

The most visible signs of the market are the indexes and averages. The most famous are the Dow, the NASDAQ Composite, and the Standard and Poor Index of 500 stocks. Each represents some portion of the total stock market and reflects the minute by minute movements of the stocks included. While none represent all of the roughly 7,000 companies publicly traded in the United States, they serve as barometers of overall investor activity. Some investors and mutual fund managers use them as benchmarks with which they can compare the performance of the particular stocks they own.

The Dow, dreamed up by journalists Charles Henry Dow and Edward Jones in 1896, is the oldest of these measures. Originally consisting of 11 stocks, it now includes 30 mighty companies known as Blue Chips. The massive decline of the Dow Jones Industrial Average in October 1929 is known to all as "The Great Crash." In the Great Depression that followed, millions of people lost their jobs and all their savings when businesses and banks closed their doors.

The movements of the Dow, the NASDAQ, and the S&P 500 signal bear markets or bull markets. When these indexes go higher and higher over a period of months, it's a bull market. When they move lower, it's a bear. Illustrations of these two kinds of markets occurred during the last 12 years of the 20th century. After more than 10 years of a record-setting bull market, especially in technology stocks, a powerful bear market swept through like a tornado in 2000 and 2001. Prices of successful as well as failing companies dropped by 50 or 60 percent. Some lost almost all their value. Those investors who had stayed on the sidelines for a few years because they thought stocks were too high missed the joy of the ride up. They also missed the pain of the ride down, and were proved correct in the end. It taught an old lesson to a new generation of investors: in the markets, as in nature, what goes up must come down.

Bugs Bunny points to a stock ticker in a window display at the Warner Brothers Studio Store in New York. The store is near the New York Stock Exchange and the running ticker keeps people updated on the market, so they can see how their investments are doing.

Stocks in the Investing Universe

People and businesses need money and will pay to use it. That makes investing possible. That's also what makes the difference between investing money and simply saving money. Investing is a way to use money to produce more money.

Saving money in a mattress or in a noninterest paying savings account is a guaranteed way to lose money. As the **cost of living** rises—and it almost always does—the dollar tends to lose value. If someone had hidden away a dollar in 1960 for example, it would have been worth about 20 cents by 2001.

Purchasing stocks is only one among many possible investments. Purchasing bonds—interest paying IOUs issued by governments and corporations—is another. A comparison of the two is useful in understanding the nature of stocks.

When you buy a share of stock, you own a stake in the company. You will probably benefit if the company does well and suffer financially if it does poorly. The management of the company owes you nothing except to work hard to make the company grow and show a profit. If they succeed, the value of the stock will increase.

When you buy a corporate bond, you are lending money to the company for a set amount of time, say 10 years. The company promises to pay you a specified rate of interest on the money loaned (the principal). When the 10 years is over, it must pay back the principal. Some shaky companies fail to live up to these obligations. But most pay their debts.

A high-grade bond comes with considerable certainty of recovering your money. In exchange for that security, the money you make, the return on your investment, is limited to the fixed interest rate. Thus bonds are fixed-income investments. You will get no extra benefit no matter how much the company may grow.

Compare this with a stock. No matter how solid the company, its shares of stock come with no guarantee of anything. It may or may not pay dividends (a share of the company's profits) to its stockholders. It may grow or shrink in value. You could lose all your money if the company goes out of business. Why, then, would anyone buy a stock instead of a bond? If the company does grow and prosper, the stock has the chance of growing a lot in value. Historically, stocks have provided a greater return to investors than bonds. But stocks are riskier because companies can do poorly or go out of business. For example, in 1903, there were 57 companies making cars. Within a few years almost half of them no longer existed.

The drive for wealth is nothing new. People have always wanted more, some for greater comfort and more material things, others for power and respect. Whenever opportunities appear, people will take a chance to profit by them, regardless of the risk. The risks may be far greater than the possible chance of succeeding, but that has never stopped them.

The gold rush is an example. In 1848 gold was discovered in California and the rush was on. In those days it took six months to sail from the east coast around South America to California. It was shorter to go overland by covered wagon, but you had to go through Indian territory and that was dangerous.

Still, almost 200,000 Americans headed for California. Many never made it. Of those who did, few found the riches they dreamed of. Yet, if a similar kind of opportunity came along today, millions of people would take the same kinds of risks chasing the same dream.

Those dreamers often had little to begin with, so they had little to lose, except their lives. But people with plenty of money may also be lured by opportunity. In the 1970s two multimillionaire brothers named Hunt had an idea: they would buy all the silver in the world. This is called cornering the market. Once they controlled all the silver, they could sell it at much higher prices to the industries like jewelry and electronics that use silver—the old law of **supply and demand** at work. The brothers borrowed enormous sums of money to carry out their scheme. They failed. Unable to repay their loans, they declared **bankruptcy.** Most of their property was taken away from them and divided up among the people to whom they owed the money.

Understanding risk and different levels of risk is essential for every investor. Experts use complicated formulas to

This is how the stock market used to work. The man standing with the gavel would call out the name of a company. Brokers would raise their hands and yell out their interest in buying or selling. Deals would be made if prices could be agreed upon. Then the chairman would call out the next name.

measure risk. But investors need only ask themselves some common sense questions: "If I invest in X, what are my chances of losing money? How much could I lose? Could I afford to lose that much?"

Generally, the investments with the potential for the greatest return are also the riskiest investments. Consider the NASCAR driver. The faster he goes, the greater his chances are of finishing first in the race. But the faster he goes, the greater too are the chances of crashing. Investing is similar.

Some investments are riskier than others. An established company with a long history of success, such as General Motors or General Electric, is less likely to produce losses for investors than a startup company with little or no profit.

It is also unlikely to grow as rapidly. Lower risk often equals lower potential return. The startup company may offer the chance of greater growth. Some have doubled or tripled in value over a period of a few years.

Careful investors follow a few basic guidelines when they think about taking a chance with their money:

1. Investors who have a small amount of money to invest try to take less risk. If you have just a little money, you can't afford to lose it all.

2. Investors with lots of money to invest try to spread it around among investments of varying risk. They might invest some in bonds, some in risky stocks, and some in less risky stocks. This is called **diversifying.**

3. The sooner an investor might need the money invested, the less risk should be taken with it. Money for a child's college tuition in three years should not be invested in a stock that goes up and down in price because it might be down, or gone, when it's needed.

Investment Clubs

Millions of Americans belong to investment clubs that they form with friends or fellow employees. They pool their money and make decisions on which stocks to buy and sell. Many of these clubs follow guidelines established by the National Association of Investment Clubs (NAIC).

Internet Cap Group, Inc.

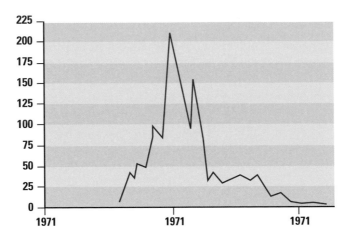

You can make a lot of money and lose a lot in the stock market, as this chart of the rapid rise and fall of Internet Cap Group, Inc. illustrates. Anyone who bought it on the way up and still has it has lost money.

Nothing about the stock market is predictable. Even well-established companies can run into serious trouble. The Xerox Company, for example, was considered one of the great technology companies in the 1970s, so dominant in the field of copiers that the brand became a verb. People still speak of "Xeroxing a document" when they mean copying a document. By the 1990s, for a variety of reasons, Xerox was in serious financial trouble. Over that period, the price of Xerox stock rose from a few dollars to $60 and then back down to $5 in 2001.

In 1998 Lucent, a telecommunications research and manufacturing company, was among the most prized stocks in the market. Then it ran into serious competitive difficulty.

Between December 1999 and mid-2001, its stock went from $80 per share to $7. Many of the best blue chip companies of the past no longer exist today. Times change. New products make old ones worthless. New technologies replace old methods. Investors must keep careful watch on their stocks because of the ever-changing fortunes of the companies they represent.

On Monday, September 17, 2001, the NYSE resumed trading for the first time since the terrorist attacks on the World Trade Center and the Pentagon six days earlier. The Dow Jones Industrial Average fell 684.81 points, the largest one-day point drop in history.

How Investors Buy and Sell Stocks

A nyone who has visited or read about bazaars in countries such as India, where they still exist, will recognize the function of the stock exchange. In a bazaar, merchants sit at stalls selling their goods. The items do not have a fixed price. Instead, the customer who strolls by asks the merchant how much he wants for the item. The merchant gives a price. The customer usually offers a lower price. If the item is not in great demand, the merchant will probably come down a little because the price offered might be the best he can get. At some point they may or may not agree on a price. If they do, the sale occurs. If many customers at the stall are interested in the same

The clothes men wear have changed, but the system of trading posts shown here in the New York Stock Exchange in 1850 is still basically the same today. Orders to buy or sell the stock of UP are still carried to the post where its stock is traded.

item—because it's rare or extremely popular—the customers themselves may bid up the price trying to outdo each other.

Stock exchanges are very much like bazaars, except the customers can't just walk into them and start shopping. They must relay their desires through stock brokers, who act as their agents.

The world's oldest continuously operating stock exchange is the London Stock Exchange in the United Kingdom. It got started in Jonathan's Coffee House, where brokers traded shares of the Muscovy Company, founded in 1553. In 1760 they changed the name of the coffee house to the Stock Exchange.

The newest (1968) large exchange, called the North American Securities Dealers Automated Quotation system (the NASDAQ) is entirely computer driven. The Philadelphia Stock Exchange, established in 1790, is the oldest in America. The New York Stock Exchange, the largest, was established in 1817 on Wall Street, which got its name from a wall built in the 17th century by the Dutch when New York was called New Amsterdam.

The first trading on Wall Street was in agricultural products and slaves. After the establishment of the United States government in 1789, groups of brokers on Wall Street bought and sold government bonds and debts of the states. The first **joint stock companies**—the early versions of publicly traded companies—began to appear in the early 1800s with the development of the first large corporations, which needed more money than just a few people could provide.

Brokers who had already been trading in these stocks informally organized the New York Stock and Exchange Board in 1817 in an attempt to bring some order to the buying and selling of shares. The operation was simple compared to the modern exchanges. An official of the board would call out the name of the company. Brokers

Bidding for Stocks

Log on to any financial web site to see the bidding process at work each day. Type in the ticker symbol in the box marked "quote" and you'll see the price at which people are willing to sell (offer), the price others will pay (bid), the price of the last trade executed, and the change in price during the day.

would respond with any buy or sell orders they wanted to place. When they agreed on a price, the deal was done and written down. The board official would then move along to the next company, going through the same motions.

Today, the New York Stock Exchange handles millions of shares of thousands of companies in a single session of continuous buying and selling that opens at 9.30 A.M. and closes with the ring of a bell at 4 P.M. The NYSE still employs trading posts on its floor, where individuals take orders to buy and sell the shares of the companies assigned to them. Only individuals who have purchased seats or memberships on the exchange can do business there. Everyone else must go through them.

It works this way. A brokerage house receives an order from one of its offices and relays it to its booth on the floor of the exchange. The broker takes the order to a trading post, where buy and sell orders in that company's stock are processed. (Sometimes brokers bump into other brokers on the floor and trade for customers among themselves rather than going to a post.) Each post has a computer display showing each transaction. Digital scanners keep track of the trades and transmit the information to an electronic

Understanding Stock Quotations

Most newspapers carry page after page of stock quotations. They show the highest price at which the stock sold by the time trading officially ended. You'll also see a low, which is the lowest price for the day. And you'll see the total volume for the day. Also listed is the high and low price for that stock over the past 52 weeks.

The spread of capitalism and free markets around the world has resulted in publicly owned companies whose stocks are traded in many countries, including Kuwait. The second largest stock market in the world today is in India, where the shares of more than 5,000 companies are traded.

tape. When the trade is complete, the broker sends a report back to the office where the order originated.

The American Stock Exchange and the NASDAQ are really networks of computers rather than people. Both are now owned by the same organization, the National Association of Securities Dealers.

How does an investor get access to the marketplace? The first step is to open an account with a stockbroker, an agent licensed to handle the dealings between buyers and sellers of stocks, just as a real estate broker negotiates the buying and selling of homes. Opening an account requires filling out forms and depositing money. You must be 18 years of age or older to open an account. Parents or guardians can open custodial accounts for younger investors. The adult is responsible for all transactions, including the payment of all bills.

Investors may choose from two basic types of brokerage firms: discount and deep discount or full service. Discount brokerages handle trades and record keeping but do not provide advice. Full service brokerages, which are more expensive, employ professional brokers and analysts who research companies and make recommendations to customers. Analysts for large brokerage houses specialize in studying different industries, such as retailing, manufacturing, technology, oil, or airlines. Both types of brokerages now generally use the Internet and the telephone as a way to communicate with clients.

Once an account is set up, the customer signs on using a password and account number. Full service brokerage customers may telephone their brokers and seek advice. An Internet-based brokerage is merely a computer network. It doesn't care whether or not you know what you're doing before you do it. Before buying or selling a stock you must know its ticker symbol, how many shares you wish to buy or sell, and the type of order to be placed: a **market order** or a **limit order.**

A market order is an order to buy or sell at the current stock price, whatever it is. It means buy—or sell—at any price. For example, if your order is executed at 2 P.M and the price at 2 P.M is $64, that's the price you'll pay if you're buying. The disadvantage of a market order is that stock prices may change swiftly, up or down. The advantage is that a market order will most likely be filled immediately.

When placing a limit order, the investor names the highest price to be paid, if buying, or the lowest acceptable price, if selling. The advantage of a limit order is that it limits the price paid or the price at which the stock is sold. But if the stock price fails to reach your limit, you won't be able to buy or sell the stock.

Through the process of placing buy and sell orders, investors are expressing their opinions about the value of different companies. An investor placing an order to buy is like that tourist at the bazaar. The shareholder wishing to sell is the equivalent of the merchant, looking for the best price.

In the bazaar, and in the stock market, there must be a willing seller for every buyer. So when you send out that buy order on a computer, you're beginning the search for a seller. Typically, the order is transmitted within seconds or minutes by the brokerage to a clearing company which handles orders from many different brokerage houses. You will have no idea who's on the other end of the transaction—which particular shareholder is willing to part with the shares you want to buy. Once a trade takes place, the investor receives a report stating the amount of money involved and when it is due. Brokerages make their money by charging a fee or commission for making the trade for you.

There are times when you can't buy or sell a stock at any price. If big news breaks about a company or a world event and too many people are trying to buy or sell at the same time, a stock exchange can stop the trading in that stock or in the entire market.

Usually these trading halts are temporary. But they can be dangerous. If you've placed a market order for a stock that many people suddenly want for some reason, the price can shoot up rapidly when trading is resumed. Or if prices collapse, your sell order could be filled at a much lower price than you expected. These events are rare, but they do happen. And they are always unexpected.

A Dell Computer Corporation employee prepares stacks of boxed computers for shipment. Many investors bought stock in Dell because of its innovative method of manufacturing. Unlike its competitors, Dell did not build any computers until it had orders for them, and then it would make them very quickly. This made the company more efficient, increasing profits.

Looking for Growth

Ownership of at least one share of a company's stock enti-
tles the shareholder to attend meetings where company
officers report on the state of the business. Stockholders are
entitled to vote on some important corporate decisions, either
in person or by mail. But in reality, small shareholders enjoy
only a small voice in the affairs of a business compared to those
who own large numbers of shares in the company. Even 1,000 or
10,000 shares of most large companies represent tiny fractions
of the whole.

Most stock investors are not interested in running companies.
They're interested in a good return on their money. Investors

can profit from stocks in two basic ways—from growth and from income. If a stock increases in value, they can sell it at a price higher than they paid and reap a profit. Someone who bought America Online in 1996 would have paid under a dollar per share. If he had sold it in late 1999, he would have gotten about $90 a share. That's real growth.

Income may also be earned from shares in companies paying dividends, a portion of the company's profits paid out to the shareholders. Older well-established companies such as gas and electric utilities tend to be income stocks. Sometimes a stock grows in price and pays dividends, too, which makes it a growth and income stock. Sometimes a stock does neither, which makes it a lemon. Newer firms engaged in the development of new products tend to use profits to grow and pay no dividends.

Dividends are distributed on a per share basis. For example, suppose a company earns a profit of $1,000 and decides to distribute $100 to shareholders in the form of dividends. If 10,000 shares are outstanding, each share would receive a dividend of a single penny. If you paid $1 for each share of the stock, the penny is a dividend of one percent.

Gambling, Not Investing

Not everyone who buys stocks is an investor. People who buy and sell stocks frequently and hold them for a short time are called traders or **speculators.** They are speculating—guessing—on the short term ups and downs of stocks with no interest in the long term growth of the company. Often they don't even care what products the company makes, or if it's earning a profit. This is gambling, not investing.

Yahoo! Inc.

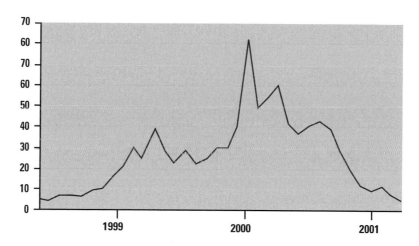

Many young computer and Internet whizzes who got in on the ground floor of the companies they worked for became millionaires when their stocks zoomed up in 1998 and 1999. Many of them became *former* millionaires just as quickly when their stocks came tumbling down.

That seems puny. But if you hold onto that stock for 10 years and it pays that penny each year, you will have received 10 percent of the original price of the stock. If you're really fortunate, a company might increase the dividend each year. Suppose that penny dividend one year is a penny and a half the next year, two pennies the third year, and so on, increasing by a half cent each year.

Your total dividend payments over 10 years will come to 32.5 cents, more than 30 percent of the money you paid for the stock. Plus you still have the stock. If the stock has also gone up during that time by 50 percent and is now worth $1.50, your investment has yielded over 80 percent (32.5 cents plus 50 cents.)

Companies regularly paying dividends used to be called "widows and orphans" stocks because they were so dependable. But no company can guarantee dividends into the future and no one can accurately predict future dividends. Income stocks seem more trustworthy than growth stocks and sometimes they are. But when the profits decline or disappear, so do the dividends.

Investors purchase growth stocks that pay no dividends in the hope the price will rise over time until it's worth more than they originally paid. A stock's price rises when investors believe the company will become worth more than its current price per share. If investors have good reason to think a stock selling for $10 a share may in the future reach $15 a share or $20 a share, they see opportunity and may consider buying it.

Many factors might lead to such a belief. Early investors in Dell Computer, for example, understood that the company had developed a more efficient method of manufacturing and selling PCs. Other computer companies attempted to estimate customer demand for their PCs in advance and then built that number—even though the result could be too many computers or too few. Dell, by comparison, built them very quickly only after a customer ordered them. That meant that Dell built only what it needed, which enabled it to purchase the computer components as needed. This reduced the chances of Dell getting stuck with large inventories of unsold computers, which could be unloaded, if at all, only by cutting prices. This increased Dell's profits. Growing profit margins made Dell an attractive investment for millions of people. Dell's ability to customize computers for each customer gave it an edge as well, increasing the company's share of all the computers sold. Growing market share also makes for an appealing investment.

Because Dell had such a successful business model, it became a great growth stock. With prices adjusted for splits, it rose from 5 cents at the end of 1989 to $1.08 per share at the end of 1995, meaning that if you'd invested a dollar at the beginning it would have been worth $20 in 1995. That's a most unusual growth rate. It could have just as easily failed, so those early investors were taking a big risk.

Thinking of companies such as Dell or Microsoft or America Online, it is too easy to forget that for every stock that performed like these, there are probably a thousand that went splat. Many investors—including some large corporations—thought in 1998 that a company developing satellite telephones had a tremendous future. But the phones turned out to be clunky and unwieldy, with reception available only when standing outside. The company, called Iridium, plunged from $60 per share to zero in little more than a year.

Performance is unpredictable in the extreme, but several basic principles have survived over the years:

1. A company with growing profits is most likely to bring solid returns to investors.

2. A company with declining profits or no profits is most likely to disappoint.

3. Any company is capable of surprising investors with good or bad news.

4. In the markets, as in life, good things tend not to last forever. Rapid growth in a stock often is followed by growth at a slower pace, or a decline.

General Electric Company

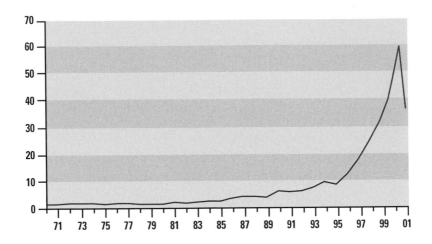

Old-fashioned, conservative investors who may have missed the booming technology stocks have done well enough with their long term investments in America's premier companies such as General Electric.

Let's look at Dell Computer again. By 1999, computer sales generally began slowing. There were too many computers on the market and not enough demand for them. Yet Dell's price remained relatively high because of its earlier success. Investors who understood early on what was happening in the PC market began selling PC stocks, including Dell's. Between the end of 1999 and the end of 2000, the price declined from $51.00 to $17.43. Perhaps Dell will rise again. But those who bought early, held on, and sold at Dell's peak made a big profit. Those investors who bought Dell in 1999 and then sold it when its price fell took a loss. Many investors still hold shares of Dell Computer. Depending on the price they paid, their Dell stock may be worth more or less than they paid for it.

The price per share of a stock alone tells you almost nothing about the value of that stock. A $600 per share stock might actually be cheaper than a $15 per share stock if the $600 stock has great profits and the $15 share has none.

Investors use various formulas to determine whether or not they consider a stock too expensive. The most widely known (it's even in ads on television) is the **price-to-earnings ratio,** or p/e ratio. It's figured by dividing the price per share by the earnings (or profits) per share. It sounds complicated, but all it's attempting to do is help investors see how much they are paying for a company's current earnings. The higher the p/e ratio, the more likely a stock is overpriced. Price-to-earnings ratios tend to soar when investors rush into a stock because of high expectations for it—often unrealistically high. Some of the technology stocks that crashed to the ground in the bear market that began in March 2000 started out with p/e ratios as high as 400. Some investors thought those stocks were overpriced: the average p/e ratio for the Standard and Poor's 500 index of stocks has historically been closer to 15.

Anyone who owns even one share of the stock of a company is entitled to go to the annual stockholders meeting, listen to the company's officials talk about the business, and ask questions, as one stockholder is doing here. Stockholders also receive regular reports, usually quarterly, from the company.

Navigating the Stock Market

If everything so far in this book makes the stock market sound like risky sailing, it is. While ordinary investors can navigate these waters and emerge alive and well, the stock market remains a challenge. Much homework and self-discipline is required to avoid losing money regularly. Much imagination is required to make money regularly.

The last chapter described how the share price of Dell Computer shot up and slid down as investors changed their attitude toward the company. In the stock market, people act on their opinions every day of the week. So the market is not merely a nonstop wealthometer, but also a nonstop opinion poll. The

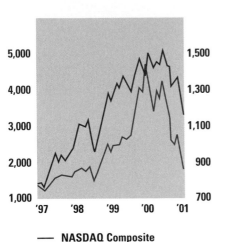

5,000
4,000
3,000
2,000
1,000

1,500
1,300
1,100
900
700

'97   '98   '99   '00   '01

—— NASDAQ Composite

—— S&P 500

This chart of the NASDAQ, which is mostly high-tech stocks, and the S&P 500, representing the stocks of 500 companies, illustrates how widespread both the rapid rise of the market and its fall have been between 1997 and 2001.

greater the demand for a stock, the higher the bidding goes over time. As demand declines, the price goes down.

The law of supply and demand controls most prices in our lives. Promoters of concerts can charge more for tickets everyone wants and less for performances by unknown groups. Someone will give you three of their Pokémon cards for just one of yours—if that one is really rare and they really want it. Stocks are more complicated because investor sentiment about the economy or any particular company is always changing.

People get panicky. They paid $10 for a stock. They see that one day it's worth $9.50 and a week later it's worth $9.00. They worry that it's going to get worse. So they try to cut their losses and sell at $9.00 per share for a $1.00 per share loss. They've bought high and sold low. It takes courage to hold stocks for the long run. But holding for the long run, if it's the right stock, allows an investor to relax a bit and avoid responding to every little change in the price as the market fluctuates.

So far we're talking about sentiment with regard to a single stock of a single company. Apply this to 100 stocks or 1,000 stocks or all stocks. Broad market sell-offs occur regularly. The fear may be based on rumor, guesswork, or unpleasant economic news stories. Sometimes fear is unexplained. Experts still argue about the cause of Black Monday, October 19, 1987, when the Dow dropped 22.6 percent.

Economic news often affects the stock market. When production is growing, and people are working and spending money, the market tends to go up in anticipation of higher corporate earnings. At such times, demand for stocks often exceeds supply, which further supports stock growth. When the economy is slowing, the market tends to decline. Then the supply of shares exceeds the demand, sending prices down.

Economic conditions influence the type of investments individuals make, too. In a slowing economy, some shift to companies providing services or products people will need regardless of economic conditions, such as soap or food. Certain events prompt some investors to shift out of stocks

Securities Fraud

Federal and state laws protect investors from fraud and cheating by officers of publicly traded companies. "Insider trading" laws, for example, punish executives and others who trade on information obtained because of their positions when it's unavailable to the public. The chief enforcement agency is the Securities and Exchange Commission (SEC), headquartered in Washington, D.C. The SEC website is www.sec.gov.

entirely, perhaps moving money into safer investments, such as government bonds. Founded or unfounded, fear has a real impact when shared by enough investors. When people see others dumping stocks rapidly, they join in the selling to protect their own money. People often act with a herd instinct; they do what they see others doing, without thinking for themselves. That happens often in the stock market. This can lead to market **panics.** Historically, panics have had little to do with any particular company and everything to do with mass psychology.

It works the other way, too. In the 1990s, millions of people bought certain stocks at high prices largely because others were buying them. They were reassured of the wisdom of their purchases because prices continued to rise even higher. The prices rose not necessarily because investors thought these companies were making profits or ever would show a profit. More likely, they rose because investors thought other investors would keep paying more for them. People operating this way are said to follow the greater fool theory. They buy stocks thinking that some greater fool will come along and buy it from them, regardless of the price. As in musical chairs, many investors get stuck at the end with worthless stocks. The result was what is called a speculative bubble. The bubble of the 1990s started losing air in March 2000, producing a dramatic decline that year of 45 percent in the Nasdaq Composite Index. Billions of dollars of stock values disappeared. People who had been millionaires one year had nothing a year later.

Mini-panics, sell-offs, and mini-booms occur regularly. You can spot them by looking at a chart of any four-month period of the Dow or NASDAQ. But if you stretch that chart out over 4 years or 14 years or 40 years, the movements seem less dramatic. That's yet another reason why holding the right stocks for a long time is a good idea. Nobody knows whether the stock market will go up or down tomorrow or next week or next year. People who are considered to be experts try to guess, but they don't really know. Anyone who tries to invest based on those guesses is as likely to lose money as to make money.

You don't have to be an expert to pick out good investments. One way is to look around you and understand what you see. Peter Lynch, a mutual fund manager for Fidelity Investments, became rich and famous during the 1980s by having a sharp eye for companies just gaining popularity with consumers. Lynch was a growth stock investor. So he studied companies primarily for their potential for growth. Visiting shopping centers he saw that a clothing store called The Limited was always crowded with young customers. He bought stock in The Limited before other investors discovered the store.

Warren Buffett, another legendary investor, specializes in value investing. He looks for companies with high potential and relatively low prices. He doesn't care if the business is glamorous or not. It could be a furniture or jewelry store, a paint company, or a candy maker. If the business is a good, solid one and has good management, he'll buy it.

Some mutual fund managers have achieved success by specializing in one industry. They become so expert in fields such as technology or health care that they sometimes know as much as the people running the businesses. Some science-related fund managers are doctors or scientists.

Other fund managers devote themselves more to mastering numbers. They specialize in analyzing companies' sales and earnings, how much cash they have, and the amount of their debt. Some look for a pattern of higher-than-expected profits each quarter. As long as the pattern continues, they hold onto a stock and maybe even buy more. When the pattern changes, they sell.

Many individual investors avoid fancy systems. They just do their own research in their own way. Knowing what a company actually does is the starting point. You may think you know already because you buy its products or see its stores in a mall. But the obvious may be only a fraction of the story. You may be interested in General Electric because you see its name on appliances in your home. But did you know it also owns NBC, CNBC, makes aircraft engines, diesel freight locomotives, plastics, and medical scanning equipment, in addition to being one of the world's largest financial services companies?

To find out what a company really owns, visit its corporate website or ask the company for a copy of its annual report to shareholders, where you can also find out how the company's earnings are doing.

Some websites now make it easy to compare the records of different companies. Some experts believe the Internet now provides too much information. An investor's challenge is distinguishing the real from the unreal. A search of any stock market ticker symbol on the Internet will produce a flood of data. But a lot of it is just gossip from chat rooms and some is made up.

In August 2000, a college student issued a fake press release about a well-known company announcing the resignation of the chief executive and a decline in profits. As a result, the share price of the company plunged from $113 to $43 in an hour. The student made thousands of dollars selling the stock short—betting his money on a drop in the stock's price. He was later arrested and prosecuted.

In September 2000, a 15-year-old boy was charged by the Securities and Exchange Commission with using numerous

Peter Kann, center, chairman and CEO of Dow Jones & Co., is joined by Richard Grasso, left, chairman and CEO of the New York Stock Exchange, and Jack Welch, chairman and CEO of General Electric Co., in 1996 to celebrate the 100th anniversary of the founding of the Dow Jones Industrial Average.

Internet chat rooms to spread exciting predictions about small companies whose stock he had bought. Other traders saw these predictions, took them seriously, and bought, pushing up the prices of the stocks. The boy then sold his shares, making thousands of dollars before he was caught.

In July 2000 a stock market TV network called CNBC got a ticker symbol wrong in a graphic. The stock of the company shown soared 75 percent in about 20 minutes. The episode provided vivid evidence that people were buying ticker symbols without even knowing the name of the company, let alone what the company did. Many investors will spend as much money on a stock as they might on a new car, but they'll do a lot more research about cars than they will about the stocks they put their money into.

Keeping track of the news is important for investors, too. Who wants to be the last to know that a business in which he owns stock has had a disaster? A typhoon or earthquake in Asia can drive the profits of American semiconductor manufacturers way up or way down because many of their factories are in Asia. Even the weather matters. A cold winter might mean higher profits for some companies and lower profits for others.

Investors or potential investors can call the investor relations department at a company that interests them and receive quite a bit of information. At a website called www.zacks.com investors can find out what professional analysts think of particular companies.

In the stock market, there is no such thing as a sure thing. Investors who are serious about stocks—and their money—try to obtain their information from reliable sources, or they rely on professional money managers to do the research for them.

The stock market was once a rich man's game, too expensive or too risky for the average person. Two developments—the popularity of mutual funds starting in the 1980s and the advent of online investing in the '90s—changed everything. For better or for worse, the rich man's game became everyman's game. And many investors chose to play it with mutual funds. Mutual fund companies pool the money of thousands, sometimes millions, of individual investors. They employ professional fund managers who buy and sell stocks on their behalf. The fund actually owns the stock. The investor owns shares of the fund.

Funds come in many varieties. Some hold a broad range of stocks and bonds. Others, such as technology funds, telecommunications funds, and health sciences funds, stick to investing in one industry. Some are income funds, others are growth funds. At the end of 2000, approximately 8,000 mutual funds were in business in the United States, half of them stock funds.

Most funds can be purchased directly from the fund company or through brokers, online and offline. Mutual funds handle the lion's share of money invested in tax-advantaged retirement accounts. Known as 401(k) and 403(b) plans when sponsored through the workplace, and Individual Retirement Accounts (IRAs) when sponsored by an individual, such accounts allow investors to defer taxes on earnings and gains until later in life.

Many investors choose to buy mutual funds because they prefer to have a professional money manager doing the buying and selling for them. They spread the risk among a great number of investments rather than concentrating it in just a few. This is especially true for investors who have small sums of money available. Two thousand dollars in a mutual fund may buy a stake in 50 to 200 different companies. The same amount invested in individual stocks directly will buy only a few shares at best. Mutual funds also provide a relatively simple method for investing in foreign stock markets.

Mutual funds have disadvantages too. They charge fees, sometimes as much as two or three percent of the value of your investment. That may seem fine if the fund has grown by 15 or 20 percent. But if it's only grown by a few percent, the fees cut the return to almost nothing and may even result in a loss of money for the investor.

Choosing among the many stock mutual funds has become almost as difficult as choosing among stocks. Growth funds concentrate on stocks with the potential for price **appreciation.** Equity-income funds focus on growth stocks and stocks paying dividends. Small cap funds invest in the stocks of smaller companies. There are companies on the Internet that allow people to build their own mutual funds. One, called FolioFn, permits individuals to purchase

Peter Lynch was one of the stars of the stock market, managing one of the most successful mutual funds in the 1970s and 1980s. Lynch was a keen observer; he would walk around shopping malls to see which stores were busy and which ones were not, then invest in those companies that were growing.

a variety of stocks in small amounts: a few shares of this, a few shares of that. Two companies doing business on the Internet, BuyAndHold.com and Sharebuilder.com, allow people to buy stocks by dollar amount rather than by numbers of shares. For example, you can invest $200 a month in four stocks, purchasing whatever amount of those stocks the money permits, a quarter share, a fifth of a share, a tenth of a share. If done regularly with the same stocks, this is similar to dollar cost averaging, where the investor purchases a little bit at a time, regardless of a stock's price. You buy some shares when prices are low and some when they're high. When the price is averaged out, the theory goes, you'll be better off than had you tried to time purchases to get the best price.

But mutual fund managers still have some advantages over the average person. They have access to new offerings—IPOs. By trading in large amounts of money, they pay less in fees and get their orders filled more swiftly at better prices. They have staffs of researchers who advise them. They are able to talk to executives of publicly traded companies to stay informed.

There's no way most investors can compete with the professionals in those ways. But there's no reason they have to compete. Successful stock market investing requires goals—and abilities—tailored to each individual. Many individuals simply choose to let the professionals do their investing for them. But the decision to begin a sound, long term investment plan, and the discipline to stick to it, is up to each person. To that extent, you are the captain of your own financial future.

Appreciation—an increase in the price of something

Aftermarket—the secondary market in which most stocks are traded after their first sale at an Initial Public Offering

Bankruptcy—a state of financial ruin

Bear Market—a period of generally falling stock prices

Bond—an IOU or note representing a loan to a company or government

Brokerage Firm—a company that fills buys and sell orders for investors

Bull Market—a period of generally rising stock prices

Capital—another term for money

Common Stock—the shares of a corporation that represent ownership of the company

Cost of living—what necessities such as food, shelter, and clothing cost in different parts of the world

Crash—a sharp decline in the stockmarket that causes many people to lose their money

Day Trader—one who buys and sells many stocks in a single day on a regular basis

Diversifying—investing in many different types of investments in order to reduce risk

Dividends—a share of profits paid to stockholders by companies

Dow Jones Industrial Average—an index of 30 leading companies listed on the New York Stock Exchange, which reflects the direction of prices of stocks in general

Great Depression—a period during the 1930s when the American economy was in severe decline, leading to widespread poverty and unemployment

Internet—a network of computers that an individual with a personal computer can tap into to view information around the world and interact with others

IPO—initial public offering of new shares of stock

Joint-stock companies—a company or association consisting of individuals organized to conduct a business for gain and having a joint stock of capital represented by shares owned individually by the members and transferable without the consent of the group

Limit order—an order to buy or sell a stock or bond that limits the price paid or the price at which the stock is sold

Market Order—an order to buy or sell a stock or bond at the best available price at the time

Mutual Fund—a pooling of money from many investors, managed by professional money managers and invested in a number of stocks or bonds

NASDAQ—a market indicator known as the North American Securities Dealers Automated Quotation System

New York Stock Exchange (NYSE)—an organization providing a place for investors' orders to be filled, and rules to govern trading activity

Panics—widespread fright concerning financial affairs that results in a depression of values

Price to earnings ratio (p/e ratio)—a formula used to determine whether a stock is overpriced; the p/e ratio is the price per share of stock divided by the earnings per share of that same stock

Prospectus—a booklet containing information about a company that is selling new shares

Securities and Exchange Commission (SEC)—a government agency regulating the investment industry

Speculator—one who buys and sells stocks, hoping for quick gains

Standard & Poor 500 (S&P 500)—a broader index than the Dow, including 500 stocks

Stocks—shares in the ownership of a company

Stock market—a place where orders to buy and sell stocks are brought together and filled by brokers acting as agents for the public; also called a stock exchange

Supply and demand—a basic rule of economics which states that when supply is low, demand and price increase; conversely, when there is an oversupply, demand is limited and price decreases

Bamford, Janet. *Street Wise: A Guide for Teen Investors.* Princeton, New Jersey: Bloomberg Press, 2000.

Edelman, Ric. *The Truth About Money.* New York: Harper Resource, 2000.

Hagstrom, Robert G. *The Warren Buffet Way: Investment Strategies of the World's Greatest Investor.* New York: John Wiley & Sons, 1997.

Lynch, Peter and John Rothchild. *Beating the Street.* Hamden, Connecticut: Fireside, 1994.

Lynch, Peter and John Rothchild. *Learn To Earn.* Hamden, Connecticut: Fireside, 1996.

Modu, Emmanuel and Andrea Walker. *The Practical Investment Guide for Teens and Their Parents.* Newark, New Jersey: Gateway, 2000.

Morris, Kenneth and Virginia B. *Your Guide to Understanding Investing.* New York: Lightbulb Press, 1999.

Schultheis, Bill. *The Coffeehouse Investor: How to Build Wealth, Ignore Wall Street, and Get On With Your Life.* Marietta, Georgia: Longstreet Press, 1998.

Smith, Pat and Lynn Roney. *Wow the Dow: The Complete Guide to Teaching Your Kids How to Invest in the Stock Market.* New York: Simon and Schuster, 2000.

Stern, Kenneth A. *Secrets of the Investing All-Stars.* Saranac Lake, New York: Amacom, 1999.

Tyson, Eric. *Investing For Dummies.* St. Paul, Minnesota: Hungry Minds, Inc., 1999.

America Online, 42, 45
American Stock Exchange, 20, 37
Antwerp, Belgium, 20
Apple, 15

Barron's, 11
Buffett, Warren, 53
Business Week, 11
BuyAndHold.com, 58

Coca-Cola, 21

Dell Computer Corp., 40,
    44–46
Dow, Charles Henry, 23

Edison, Thomas, 12

Fidelity Investments, 53
Financial Times, 11
FolioFn, 57
Ford, Henry, 15, 17–18
Ford Motor Co., 18
Fortune, 11

General Electric, 28, 54
General Motors, 28
Gold rush, 27
Great Depression, 8, 23

Hewlett Packard, 15

India, 33
Investors Business Daily, 11

Jonathan's Coffee House, 34
Jones, Edward, 23

Kellogg, 21
Krispy Kreme Doughnuts, Inc., 15

London Stock Exchange, 34
Lucent, 30–31
Lynch, Peter, 53, 58

Microsoft, 45
Money, 11
Muscovy Company, 34

NASDAQ, 20, 35, 37
National Association of
    Investment Clubs, 29
New York Stock Exchange, 20, 25,
    35, 36

Online trading, 9–11
Online Trading Academy.Com, 10

Philadelphia Stock Exchange, 35

Schwab, Charles, Co., 10, 11
Securities and Exchange
    Commission, 16, 51, 54
Sharebuilder.com, 58
SmartMoney, 11

The Limited, 53

Wall Street Journal, 11
Wal-Mart, 21

Xerox, 30

page
2: Associated Press/Wide World Photos
6: Associated Press/Wide World Photos
9: Library of Congress
10: Associated Press/Wide World Photos
12: Library of Congress
14: Associated Press/Wide World Photos
17: Choptank Syndicate
19: New York Public Library
20: New York Public Library
24: Associated Press/Wide World Photos
28: Library of Congress

30: Choptank Syndicate
32: Associated Press/Wide World Photos
34: New York Public Library
37: Associated Press/Wide World Photos
40: Associated Press/Wide World Photos
43: Choptank Syndicate
46: Choptank Syndicate
48: Associated Press/Wide World Photos
50: Choptank Syndicate
55: Associated Press/Wide World Photos
58: Associated Press/Wide World Photos

FRED BARBASH is a Washington writer. He retired from *The Washington Post* in July 2001 after 25 years at the paper, most recently as the paper's investing columnist and business editor. He has served as the *Post*'s National Editor, Chief of the London Bureau, and U.S. Supreme Court correspondent. He is the author of *The Founding: A Dramatic Account of the Writing of the Constitution*, Simon and Schuster, 1987.